Introduction:

This booklet contains a full practice exam, written to provide you with the practice experience needed to prepare for the actual exam. This practice exam should help you see whether you have not only memorized your study material but are also able to apply it, which is the only way to pass the exam.

There are 90 questions, distributed over 18 cases. The score to aim for is 80% correct, meaning 18 mistakes or fewer. If you scored 80% or higher, consider yourself ready for exam day.

How to take this practice exam:

Take a piece of paper, a pencil, and a timer. Set the timer for 2.5 hours. Write down the number of the question and the answer you think is correct. If you do not immediately know the correct answer, or you would like to review your answer at the end, write a question mark behind that question. This indicates that you flagged the answer for later review, so you do not waste time if you are stuck (very useful during the actual exam as well!).

Afterward, go to the answer section of this booklet. The answer key is provided, which allows you to determine your score. An explanation is provided in the last section of this booklet. Keep in mind that it is important to understand the logic behind the questions and answers, since that is one of the benefits of using this practice exam.

About this document:

The practice exams currently available are incomplete, expensive, and treacherously easy. This practice exam provides you with more of a challenge than the alternatives. The brief explanations should help you understand the way questions can be phrased and how to choose the best answer.

After using this booklet as intended, combined with your regular study material, you should have improved your speed and accuracy, leaving you with sufficient time to go back to review the questions you flagged.

The topics and types of questions in this practice exam are balanced to resemble the actual exam. However, if you would like to test your skills in applying the GDPR further than this practice exam, please try "European Privacy Law Practice Exam: Case study Edition", which contains material to focus specifically on the scenario question part of the exam (which will be the most difficult part of the exam) and provides more of a challenge to test whether you really understand the GDPR.

Good luck!

Kind regards,

Jasper Jacobs, CIPP/E, CIPP/US, CIPM, CIPT

EXAM QUESTIONS:

1. What kind of right is privacy in the context of article 8 of the European Convention of Human rights?
A. An absolute right
B. More important than the freedom of others
C. Not an absolute right
D. Freedom to impart ideas onto others

2. Which treaty established the European Economic Community?
A. The treaty of Paris
B. The treaty of Rome
C. The treaty of Maastricht
D. The treaty of Lisbon

3. Which European institution audits the European Union?
A. The European Parliament
B. The European Council
C. The European Central Bank
D. The European Court of Auditors

4. Which of the following is the executive body of the European Union?
A. The European Court of Auditors
B. The European Parliament
C. The European Council
D. The European Commission

5. Which of the following are the two important European Privacy laws?
A. The Children Online Privacy Protection Act and the Protection of Personal Information Act
B. The European Convention of Human Rights and the Data Retention Directive
C. Binding Corporate Rules and Standard Contractual Clauses
D. The General Data Protection Regulation and the e-Privacy directive

6. Which directive or law is the most likely document referred to by a Data Protection Officer for marketing via e-mail?
A. The General Data Protection Regulation
B. The European Convention on Human Rights
C. The Data Protection Directive
D. The e-Privacy directive

7. What is the most fitting definition of *personal data*?
A. Data stored in a filing system
B. Data subject to automated processing
C. Anything that says something about an identifiable person
D. Information manifestly made public

8. Who determines the purpose and means of processing?
A. The processor
B. The controller
C. The data subject
D. The Data Protection Authority

9. When are data considered to be anonymous?
A. When the names and addresses have been removed
B. When the data are encrypted
C. When no breach has occurred
D. When the data cannot be traced back to an individual

10. Which of the following is considered a data subject?
A. An identifiable person about whom information is stored
B. A company subject to a Data Protection Agency's investigation
C. An anonymous person wishing no data is collected about him/her
D. A European corporation operating within the European Economic Area

11. Which of the following can be considered a processor?
A. An insurance company with a database of 20,000 customers
B. A flower shop maintaining a list of home addresses at the request of one of his corporate customers
C. A cloud service, offering its services to private customers
D. A data broker, selling anonymized data it collected on its own initiative

12. When does the GDPR apply to a US-based company?
A. When the company's .com website attracts European customers, buying American flags
B. When the company employs EU citizens
C. When the company targets EU citizens or processes personal data in the European Union
D. When the company's website is visited by European citizens

13. Who does the GDPR most likely apply to?
A. A German individual, collecting and storing social media information of his wife, who he suspects is cheating on him because their newborn baby looks nothing like him
B. A Greek government agency, publishing a list of persons deceased in a recent natural disaster
C. A researcher of a Belgian university, researching an indigenous tribe in Papoa New Guinnes
D. A Spanish agency, keeping a list of all corporations in the region

14. An organization is selling candy from within Europe by mail order. Does the GDPR apply?
A. Yes, because the candy is shipped within the European Union
B. Yes, it handles customers, which most likely results in the processing of personal data
C. No, because candy is not personal data
D. No, because a privacy notice is provided

15. To which extent is the GDPR applicable to Canadian direct marketing companies targeting EU citizens?
A. The e-Privacy directive does not apply outside of the European Union, hence there is no regulation of direct marketing
B. Only appropriate data security safeguards are required, no administrative safeguards
C. Canadian marketing requires approval of the Canadian privacy ombudsman
D. The GDPR applies to the activities targeting EU citizens

16. Which of the following is an example of the application of the storage limitation principle?
A. Denying data subjects access after the data are no longer needed
B. Making sure the data are accurate before destroying the data
C. Not storing personal data longer than necessary for the purposes for which the data were collected
D. Performing regular audits to verify not more data than needed have been collected

17. Which of the following is an example of the purpose limitation principle?
A. Vetting contractors before allowing them access to the data
B. Using the personal data only for the purpose for which the data were collected
C. Using encryption methods suitable for the processing purpose
D. Denying the Corporate Information Security Officer access to the processing description

18. Which of the following is an example of the application of confidentiality?
A. Information is only shared with the persons that need to have access to the required information for use in line with the purpose for which it was collected
B. Only publicly available personal data being used
C. Not storing any names in the collection process
D. Providing a privacy notice before collecting the data

19. Which of the following is an example of the application of the concept accuracy?
A. Allowing data subjects to correct their data when there is a change
B. Making sure the data stay the way they were collected, regardless of data subject signals
C. Preventing data breaches that allow outsiders to access the data
D. Requiring consent for the processing of the data

20. When is consent most likely not required?
A. When it concerns digital marketing surveys for children, with a reward at the end
B. When it concerns public sensitive data
C. When it concerns processing where no other lawful processing criterion applies
D. When it concerns data that are nice to have, but not essential for the purpose, and it differs per person whether the interests of the controller outweigh the interests of the data subject

21. When is article 6b of the GDPR, processing for a contract of which the data subject is a part, applicable?
A. When installing CCTV in order to keep customers safe
B. When processing a CV and other required applicant details in the recruitment process
C. When processing your employees' data in the process of organizing the annual corporate family event
D. When posting the photograph of individuals that have stolen from your shop

22. When is article 6c of the GDPR, compliance with a legal obligation the controller is subject to, applicable?
A. When a school stores its potential student's addresses after sending a leaflet with information because it is legally required to provide information on the educational options it provides
B. When posting CCTV images of individuals that have stolen from your shop
C. When a school records the national personal identification number, as required by law
D. When asking a patient for consent to send him/her information regarding the medication he/she is taking

23. Which lawful processing criterion would you most likely use if you are asked access to provide the medical file of one of your employees by an ambulance that needs the information to treat the employee (who fell unconscious)?
A. Vital interest
B. Performance of a contract
C. Task carried out in the public interest
D. Consent (sensitive personal data)

24. Which of the following is the best example of the application of the transparency principle?
A. Asking for specific consent after collecting personal data
B. Requiring consent as a condition for using a website
C. Informing data subjects of their rights of erasure
D. Providing a privacy notice explaining what is done with the collected data, by who and why

Use this scenario for the following four questions:

A supermarket has a discount card which is provided free to its customers. In order to receive a discount for specific products, customers hand over the discount cart at the cash register, after which it is scanned and the discount is applied.

Besides the card being used to provide a discount, it also registers all items purchased by the user of the discount card. Through a website, users can register the card and link it to themselves in order to receive personalized discount offers, based on their shopping preferences.

The supermarket's new data protection officer has just started to familiarize himself with the discount card and the processes behind it. During his efforts to fully explore the process, he finds out no privacy notice is provided to the customers before linking their name and e-mail address to the discount card. Somewhat alarmed by this discovery, he plans a meeting with the manager in charge of the discount card rollout.

25. When should the privacy notice be provided to the customers using the discount card?
A. Before storing the name and e-mail address
B. Before asking the customer for his/her name and e-mail address
C. Before issuing the discount card
D. Before sending any personalized discounts to the customer, since this is considered marketing

26. What is required to be part of the privacy notice for the discount card?
A. The names and addresses of the processors used
B. The lawful processing criteria
C. The names and addresses of the sub-processors used
D. The population size of the data subjects

27. Which of the following is an example of a layered privacy notice?
A. A privacy notice on each sub-section of a website, so that the notice is always visible
B. A notice with reference to another privacy policy so that not all information is contained in just one notice
C. A notice with the contact details of the general council as well as the privacy council so that more specific communication can take place
D. A notice in which a section can be unfolded for every area of interest, such as for marketing

28. Which of the following elements is not required in the discount card privacy notice?
A. Contact details of the Data Protection Officer
B. A mention of who the controller is
C. A description of third parties involved
D. The contact person at the Data Protection Agency

29. Which of the following is not true regarding fair processing notices?
A. Fair processing notices are held to more elaborate requirements since the GDPR
B. It is mandatory, where possible, to provide a fair processing notice before collecting personal data
C. The Data Protection Directive already specified methods for controllers to provide fair processing notices
D. The identification of the controller needs to be included in a fair processing notice

30. What is true for third parties collecting personal data on behalf of a controller?
A. Neither the identity nor the contact details are required to be disclosed to the data subjects
B. The controller is exempt from the requirement to identify itself because a processor is in charge of determining the means and purpose of the collection
C. On request, the data processing agreement needs to be made available to the data subjects
D. Third parties are required to identify the controller for which the personal data are collected

31. Which of the following is most appropriate when it concerns technologies that provide fair processing notice challenges, such as CCTV?
A. When it is difficult to provide a fair processing notice due to the type of technology used, the most appropriate way of delivering the information in the context of the technology has to be sought
B. Difficult technologies are exempt from the requirement to provide a fair processing notice, due to the expense of the organization outweighing the data subject's right to privacy
C. CCTV is only allowed to be used with consent, meaning the fair processing notice can be provided at the same moment consent is provided
D. Difficulties need to be reported to the European Data Protection Board for approval

32. How long does an organization initially have to respond to a data subject's access request?
A. One month
B. 20 days
C. 35 days
D. 10 days

33. When can an organization refuse to comply with a request from a data subject to delete his/her personal data?
A. When the organization has not yet appointed a Data Protection Officer
B. During a busy period, an organization can refuse the request and tell the data subject he/she has to file the request again in three months
C. When there is a legal obligation to keep the data
D. When no objection has taken place at the moment of collection

34. When a data subject wishes to make use of his/her right to data portability, which of the following applies?
A. The controller has the right to prevent a data subject from providing the personal data to another controller
B. The personal data have to be provided in machine-readable format
C. The right to data portability includes non-personal data
D. A data subject wishing to make use of his/her right to data portability is obliged to provide a safe means of transferring the data, e.g. an encrypted USB drive

Use this scenario for the following three questions:

A high school has received a request from Eric, who claims to be a recent graduate. Eric has started preparing his application for a scientific grant for an undergraduate research project he wants to start. In order to complete the application, he needs a transcript of his high school grades. The school still has the transcript, which it is required by law to keep for seven years.

35. What should the school do with the request?
A. Tell Eric that he was under 16 years of age at the time he attended the school, hence only his parents can be granted access
B. Ask Eric to provide identification, to make sure he is who he says he is
C. Grant the request, since the GDPR allows exceptions for scientific research
D. Refuse the request, since access requests can only be made in person

36. If Eric, upon realizing how poor his grades were, requests erasure of the transcript (since it concerns his personal data), what should the school do?
A. Refuse the erasure of the transcript
B. Require Eric to sign a deletion request statement, as a place holder for any legal requirement
C. Grant the request, since the GDPR gives data subjects the right to be forgotten
D. Inform Eric that only his parents are able to authorize the school to delete the transcript

37. If, after refusal of access, Eric hacks the school's IT system and gains access to his transcript, which of the following is most likely the case?
A. It is fine, as Eric is merely executing his rights
B. The data have to be deleted, as required by law
C. It constitutes a data breach
D. Eric has forfeited his rights to erasure

38. What is the best example of appropriate technical and organizational measures?
A. The highest standards of IT security, with automatic updates enabled
B. Security measures appropriate for the level of risk that the processing poses, periodically re-evaluated
C. What the salesperson recommends, if you do not trust the Chief Information Security Officer's demands
D. Procedures and equipment that ensure full encryption and access to data through a single person only

39. What is required when contracting an external company to perform payroll operations?
A. A Data Processing Agreement
B. Binding Corporate Rules
C. Approval from the Data Protection Authority
D. If the services were provided before 2016, no additional actions are required

40. What is likely the most appropriate first step after discovering a potential data breach?
A. Starting an investigation into what exactly has been breached
B. Filing a claim against any processor at fault
C. Calling the Data Protection Authority to request help with the investigation
D. Informing all data subjects that your organization holds data on

41. If a processor that you have contracted reports a data breach to you (the controller), what actions are required of you?
A. Record the breach, and potentially report it to the Data Protection Authority
B. The processor is responsible, and therefore the only one to take action
C. No action is required of the controller, as there are Binding Corporate Rules in place
D. No action is required of the controller, as there is a Data Processing Agreement in place

42. How fast is a controller required to report a severe breach to the Data Protection Authority?
A. 24 hours after finishing the investigation
B. 72 hours after having become aware of the breach
C. 24 hours after informing the involved data subjects
D. 48 hours

43. If you are a processor, do you need a Data Processing Agreement for any sub-processors that you use?
A. No, any sub-processor you hire is automatically liable for complying with the Data Processing Agreements you are part of
B. Sub-processors never require a Data Processing Agreement
C. A processor is not allowed to use sub-processors, as these are required to be contracted directly through the controller
D. Yes, the Data Processing Agreement does not automatically apply to sub-processors

44. Which of the following would most likely require a Data Processing Agreement?
A. A flower service, delivering flowers to your personal address
B. A catering service, asked to provide three gluten-free meals for a company event
C. The company leasing you IT hardware for your organization
D. A cloud provider where the minutes of meeting of all meetings of your organization are stored

45. Within what time does a processor have to inform a controller after becoming aware of a Data Breach?
A. Within 72 hours after having become aware of it
B. 48 hours
C. 24 hours
D. Without undue delay after becoming aware of a personal data breach

46. What is the most likely situation in which communication to the data subjects needs to take place?
A. An e-mail has been wrongfully addressed and contains someone's refugee status
B. Thousands of IP addresses, of persons who responded to a digital marketing survey, have been published
C. An encrypted laptop with a kill switch has been lost, leaving the backup as the only copy
D. A drawer containing a variety of documents, including business cards containing personal data randomly, spread out through the drawer, has been accessed by the after-hours cleaner

47. Which of the following is most accurate regarding security?
A. A controller is responsible for the security of its processing, but can shift this responsibility by outsourcing it to a processor
B. A data processor is held to different security standards than a controller
C. Processor and controller both need to be able to prove they are processing with an appropriate level of security
D. No duty to inspect red flags lies with the contractor, as long as a data processing agreement has been signed

48. Which of the following does not constitute a data breach?
A. A wrongfully addressed e-mail containing personal data
B. The accidental destruction of a securely encrypted hard drive containing personal data, which has not been backed up
C. A fully encrypted laptop containing personal data being stolen
D. Processing personal data without the required data processing agreement

49. What is not a good example of *privacy by design*?
A. Having the option to select "Do not Track" in a browser
B. Making sure as little information as needed is collected within a website
C. Automatically disabling analytical and tracking cookies
D. Making sure no connection with the internet is made if it is not needed

50. When is a Data Protection Impact Assessment most likely required?
A. When re-performing a high-risk process, with different data subjects
B. When installing additional CCTV cameras
C. When developing an application for minors with a terminal illness, which they can use on their smartphone to assist in their therapy
D. When working with anonymized ultra-sensitive data

51. What is the best description of a Data Protection Impact Assessment?
A. A risk assessment used to come to an estimate on the needed financial resources
B. An assessment of the impact of the processing operations on the protection of personal data
C. A mandatory document for all types of processing
D. A mandatory document for high-risk data, regardless of whether the high-risk data are personal data

52. In which of the following cases is a Data Protection Officer not mandatory?
A. Courts acting in their judicial capacity
B. Public authorities
C. When a company engages in regular and systematic monitoring of data subjects on a large scale
D. When the core activities of the organization consist of the processing on a large scale of special categories of personal data

53. What is not required of the Data Protection Officer?
A. Inform and advise the organization of its data protection obligations
B. Monitor compliance with the GDPR
C. Accept dismissal or penalization for the performance of his/her tasks
D. Report breaches to the Data Protection Authority

54. What is the predecessor of Privacy Shield?
A. HIPAA
B. The CLOUD Act
C. Safe Harbor
D. Binding Corporate Rules

55. What is the best description of *standard contractual clauses*?
A. A framework for transatlantic exchanges of personal data for commercial purposes between the European Union and Canada
B. Model clauses for personal data exchanges with countries outside the European Union
C. A framework for transatlantic exchanges of personal data for commercial purposes between the European Union and the rest of the world
D. It is an inter-company agreement, with at least one of the affiliates based in the United States, with approval of the designated Data Protection Authority

56. What is the best description of Binding Corporate Rules?
A. A document describing the internal reprimanding of employees involved in data breaches
B. Any international document for which the Data Protection Officer has given his/her approval
C. A slimmed-down version of the standard contractual clauses
D. A legally binding document applicable to every member of a group's undertaking

57. Which of the following countries is not considered adequate (moment of writing, August 2020)?
A. New Zealand
B. Jersey
C. Guernsey
D. Australia

58. When would standard contractual clauses for international data transfer be used (moment of writing, August 2020)?
A. When transferring data to a government agency in Canada
B. When using the service of a processor in Israel
C. When transferring to another affiliate of the same organization in a country that has not been found adequate, with Binding Corporate Rules in place
D. When transferring substantial anonymized data to a country with a recent high-profile data breach

59. What is not true about standard contractual clauses?
A. When used instead of Binding Corporate Rules, each legal entity of a group has to sign the standard contractual clauses
B. Clauses can be freely adjusted to fit the specifics of the exchange
C. The clauses cannot be altered freely
D. The Data Protection Authority does not need to authorize the use of unaltered standard contractual clauses

60. Which of the following is still necessary for the transfer of personal data to a country with an adequacy decision?
A. Binding Corporate Rules
B. Model clauses
C. Alternative Transfer mechanisms
D. A Data Processing Agreement, in case of processors and sub-processors

61. Which of the following is true for Binding Corporate Rules?
A. They have to be approved by the Data Protection Officer
B. They have to be part of a Data Processing Agreement
C. They have to be approved by the Data Protection Authority
D. They replace the need for a Data Processing Agreement

62. Who determines whether a country has an adequate level of protection?
A. The European Data Protection Supervisor
B. The Data Protection Authority
C. The European Commission
D. The country's privacy ombudsperson or commissioner

63. At the moment of the drafting of the GDPR, which of the possibilities it provides was new?
A. Standard contractual clauses for international data transfer
B. Sub-processor contract requirements
C. Codes of conduct for international data transfer
D. Controller to controller standard contractual clauses

64. For multinational organizations, what is true regarding where their Data Protection Authority is located?
A. Multinational organizations only answer to the European Data Protection Supervisor
B. Multinational organizations only answer to the European Data Protection Board
C. Multinational organizations fall outside of the scope of the GDPR, provided that their head office is in a country that has been deemed adequate
D. The supervisory authority of the main/single establishment of the controller/processor shall be competent to act as the lead supervisory authority

65. What is not a role of the Data Protection Authority?
A. Promote awareness and understanding of data protection
B. Handle complaints and carry out investigations
C. Provide tools and templates for GDPR implementation
D. Monitor development of ICT and commercial practices

66. What is the name of the predecessor of the European Data Protection Board?
A. European Data Protection Supervisor
B. Safe Harbor Council
C. Article 29 Working Party
D. Privacy Shield Council

67. What is true regarding the European Data Protection Board?
A. It is, among others, composed of the head of one supervisory authority of each member state
B. The opinions issued by the European Data Protection Board are fully enforceable as law
C. The European Data Protection Board issues revisions of the GDPR, as needed
D. The European Data Protection Board, due to its authority and expertise, has the power to overturn any judge-made decision

68. What is true about the possible fines under the GDPR?
A. The maximum fine is 2% of the total worldwide annual turnover of the previous year, or 10 Million Euros
B. The maximum fine is 10 Million Euros for companies operating on a national level, and 20 Million Euros for a company operating on a global level
C. There is no maximum fine
D. The maximum fine is 4% of the total worldwide annual turnover of the previous year, or 20 Million Euros

69. Which of the following is not one of the supervisory authority's investigative powers?
A. To carry out investigations in the form of data protection audits
B. To carry out a review on certifications that demonstrate compliance
C. To fine individuals for not cooperating with an investigation
D. To obtain access to any premises of the controller and the processor

70. What is true regarding the compensation mentioned in article 82 of the GDPR?
A. Limited to a maximum of 4% of the global annual turnover or 20 Million Euros
B. The damage can be material or non-material
C. Limited to a maximum of 2% of the global annual turnover
D. Limited to 10 Million euros

71. What is the most likely legal basis for processing employee data?
A. The data subject has given consent
B. The data subject has implied consent
C. Necessary in order to protect the vital interests of the data subject
D. Necessary for the performance of a contract

72. What is true about workplace monitoring?
A. In order not to upset the employees, the cameras should be hidden
B. Approval from the Data Protection Authority is required
C. A privacy notice is required
D. Explicit consent is always required

73. Which of the following is most likely a safeguard in place when an organization allows employees to use personal devices for work?
A. Provide budget for procuring devices
B. Mandatory cloud backups of the entire device's content
C. Establish a Bring Your Own Device policy
D. Exclusion of employee devices from the data inventory

Use this scenario for the following three questions:

Company X is the market leader in the production of diet pills. It has a facility in Sweden, which employs 1200 people full time. Recently, it invented a drug that speeds up metabolism. This drug's formula is something company X wants to keep a secret for as long as possible.

In the coming months company X plans on expanding its manufacturing facility to create space for the production of its newest diet pill. Heavy use will be made of CCTV, especially in the critical production areas where the ingredients are mixed.

Before being allowed to work for company X, employees are informed of the use of CCTV. However, the new manufacturing area raises concerns. The works council requested an urgent meeting with the board of directors and the Data Protection Officer.

74. What is the role of an organization's works council with regards to privacy in the case of company X?
A. Works councils are mostly active in the UK, and company X is based in Sweden, hence the works council is likely going to have little power
B. Works councils are always required to be asked for approval for any privacy-related issues, so also in this case
C. The works council could be involved if privacy issues are the result of changes in the work environment
D. Works councils are responsible for the development of a whistle-blowing scheme, which makes CCTV redundant and disproportionate

75. Company X is not asking its employees for consent for the use of CCTV. What is most likely the reason not to ask its employees for consent?
A. Because it would be difficult to be truly freely given
B. Because of the large number of consent forms
C. Because employers only process employee data based on legitimate interest
D. Because employers only process employee data for the vital interest of employees

76. Besides the use of CCTV, there are other personal data that company X processes of its employees, potentially of a sensitive nature. When are sensitive personal data about employees allowed to be processed without consent?
A. When compensation is provided for the use of the personal data
B. When the name of the employee is replaced with a code, and the list with names belonging to the codes is kept separately
C. When the processing is carried out in the legitimate interest of the organization
D. When it is necessary for carrying out obligations in the field of employment law

77. Which of the following is most likely true for an employer installing CCTV throughout the organization's premises?
A. The legitimate interest criterion is used and privacy notices are visible before entering the premises
B. The works councils have no right to provide input regarding the decision to place CCTV
C. Employers are allowed to do as they please, since coming to work is voluntary
D. Employees can request to see the recordings of all their colleagues based on their right to access

78. What is necessary for the use of geolocation tracking of employees?
A. It needs to be proportional and necessary
B. The geolocation of employees does not fall under the category personal data
C. Geolocation tracking is only allowed if vehicles are tracked, and not employees
D. Within Europe, geolocation tracking is allowed without any restrictions

79. What is required when sending digital direct marketing?
A. A prior customer relationship and the opportunity to opt out
B. A data broker's list of contacts
C. Social media profile information
D. Any list provided by a third party from outside of the European Economic Area

80. What is required when sending direct marketing via old-fashioned snail mail?
A. Works council approval
B. A legitimate interest and a prior customer relationship
C. A follow up e-mail with the request for a confirmation of receipt
D. Approval from the Data Protection Authority

81. Which of the following is not true regarding web beacons?
A. Web beacons can be third-party trackers
B. Opt-out is sufficient, which can be provided through changing the browser settings
C. More than just the IP address can be collected when using a web beacon
D. The use of a third-party web beacon for profiling most likely requires consent

82. When targeting children under 13 for an online survey, which of the following is most likely required?
A. The option to opt-out
B. The option to omit the child's address
C. Parental consent
D. A contract with the child

83. Which of the following is true regarding the use of photos of members of your organization for marketing purposes?
A. Using your employees' photographs is considered necessary for the performance of their employment contract
B. If your organization's members are recognizable, you will most likely require consent for the use of the photograph for marketing purposes
C. Works council approval is required
D. Only photographs that are also posted on social media are allowed to be used for marketing purposes

84. Which of the following is true regarding the use of publicly available data for marketing purposes?
A. Publicly available information falls outside of the scope of the GDPR
B. For any processing of publicly available information, one of the lawful processing criteria will have to be met
C. When first processing the publicly available information outside of Europe, it will fall outside of the scope of the GDPR
D. Only information publicly available in Europe falls under the scope of the GDPR

85. What is the best description of cloud computing?
A. The hosting of intranet pages that are not accessible to outsiders
B. The use of dynamic IP addresses
C. Any storage of data on an externally hosted server
D. Phone towers connecting individual devices

86. Which of the following types of cookies least likely requires consent?
A. Tracking cookies
B. Web beacons
C. Functional Cookies
D. Analytical cookies

87. Regarding social networks, which of the following is most likely true?
A. Any processing a social media site does falls under personal use
B. Only the processing of photos depicting race or physical impairment requires consent
C. An individual is always regarded to have provided valid implicit consent
D. Consent is required for organizations to transfer personal data to social networks for marketing purposes

88. Which of the following is true regarding search engine operators?
A. Data retention periods must be proportional
B. Search engine operators require consent before processing search commands
C. Search engines are always considered to be processors
D. Search engines fall outside the scope of the GDPR

89. Which of the following is most likely true regarding a well-known social media site's practice of labeling its members' sexual preferences based on their online behavior?
A. Any online behavior is manifestly made public, so any conclusions regarding sexual preference attached to it do not require consent
B. The website needs to obtain consent to record a prediction/inference of someone's sexual preference
C. Inference is fine, as it is not 100% certain to be accurate
D. Unless the data subject objects, the accuracy principle is not enforceable since the data are not presented as accurate

90. Which of the following is not true regarding privacy notices and social media?
A. The privacy notice needs to be concise and in an easily accessible form
B. Transparency is a requirement of the privacy notice
C. The privacy notice always needs to be intelligible
D. The consequences of actions on social media are commonly known, and for that reason do not require a privacy notice

CORRECT ANSWERS:

1C	31A	61C
2B	32A	62C
3D	33C	63C
4D	34B	64D
5D	35B	65C
6D	36A	66C
7C	37C	67A
8B	38B	68D
9D	39A	69C
10A	40A	70B
11B	41A	71D
12C	42B	72C
13C	43D	73C
14B	44D	74C
15D	45D	75A
16C	46A	76D
17B	47C	77A
18A	48D	78A
19A	49A	79A
20B	50C	80B
21B	51B	81B
22C	52A	82C
23A	53C	83B
24D	54C	84B
25B	55B	85C
26B	56D	86C
27D	57D	87D
28D	58A	88A
29C	59B	89B
30D	60D	90D

QUESTIONS WITH BRIEF EXPLANATIONS:

1. What kind of right is privacy in the context of article 8 of the European Convention of Human rights?
A. An absolute right
B. More important than the freedom of others
C. Not an absolute right (correct)
D. Freedom to impart ideas onto others
Explanation: the right to privacy is balanced against other rights.

2. Which treaty established the European Economic Community?
A. The treaty of Paris
B. The treaty of Rome (correct)
C. The treaty of Maastricht
D. The treaty of Lisbon
Explanation: this is what B established. The others did not.

3. Which European institution audits the European Union?
A. The European Parliament
B. The European Council
C. The European Central Bank
D. The European Court of Auditors (correct)
Explanation: the court of auditors is the external audit agency of the EU, and the name gives away that they mainly perform audits.

4. Which of the following is the executive body of the European Union?
A. The European Court of Auditors
B. The European Parliament
C. The European Council
D. The European Commission (correct)
Explanation: as likely mentioned in your textbook, the Commission is the executive body that implements policies/decisions and monitors compliance.

5. Which of the following are the two important European Privacy laws?
A. The Children Online Privacy Protection Act and the Protection of Personal Information Act
B. The European Convention of Human Rights and the Data Retention Directive
C. Binding Corporate Rules and Standard Contractual Clauses
D. The General Data Protection Regulation and the e-Privacy directive (correct)
Explanation: the GDPR is obvious, but the e-Privacy directive may already have been replaced. Keep this way of phrasing questions in mind, as there may be outdated references in the exam.

6. Which directive or law is the most likely document referred to by a Data Protection Officer for marketing via e-mail?
A. The General Data Protection Regulation
B. The European Convention on Human Rights
C. The Data Protection Directive
D. The e-Privacy directive (correct)
Explanation: although the GDPR also applies, the e-Privacy directive has specific requirements for electronic communications.

7. What is the most fitting definition of *personal data*?
A. Data stored in a filing system
B. Data subject to automated processing
C. Anything that says something about an identifiable person (correct)
D. Information manifestly made public
Explanation: C is the definition of personal data. A, B & C refer to criteria that determine how personal data should be treated, but are themselves not part of a definition of personal data.

8. Who determines the purpose and means of processing?
A. The processor
B. The controller (correct)
C. The data subject
D. The Data Protection Authority
Explanation: B, simple. A, C and D influence the purpose and means, perhaps, but do not determine them.

9. When are data considered to be anonymous?
A. When the names and addresses have been removed
B. When the data are encrypted
C. When no breach has occurred
D. When the data cannot be traced back to an individual (correct)
Explanation: only D is correct. The other options do not necessarily prevent the data from being traced back to someone. B may seem tricky, but encrypting something does not irreversibly remove identifiers.

10. Which of the following is considered a data subject?
A. An identifiable person about whom information is stored (correct)
B. A company subject to a Data Protection Agency's investigation
C. An anonymous person wishing no data is collected about him/her
D. A European corporation operating within the European Economic Area
Explanation: only A directly allows identification of a natural person, which is a data subject. C could technically also be correct with certain reasoning, but that is not the logic you will find on the exam.

11. Which of the following can be considered a processor?
A. An insurance company with a database of 20,000 customers
B. A flower shop maintaining a list of home addresses at the request of one of his corporate customers (correct)
C. A cloud service, offering its services to private customers
D. A data broker, selling anonymized data it collected on its own initiative
Explanation: the flower shop keeps personal data at the request of a company, so it is a processor (the company determines the means and purpose). The correct answer is B. A is a controller, C is only offering to private customers (so likely not to controllers), and D is not collecting on behalf of a controller.

12. When does the GDPR apply to a US-based company?
A. When the company's .com website attracts European customers, buying American flags
B. When the company employs EU citizens
C. When the company targets EU citizens or processes personal data in the European Union (correct)
D. When the company's website is visited by European citizens
Explanation: C is correct, since the company actively targets them. In the other options, the assumption is that the company does not actively target them. During the exam, make assumptions this way if the answer otherwise is not clear or logical.

13. Who does the GDPR most likely apply to?
A. A German individual, collecting and storing social media information of his wife, who he suspects is cheating on him because their newborn baby looks nothing like him
B. A Greek government agency, publishing a list of persons deceased in a recent natural disaster
C. A researcher of a Belgian university, researching an indigenous tribe in Papoa New Guinnes (correct)
D. A Spanish agency, keeping a list of all corporations in the region
Explanation: C is the correct answer because the Belgian university is a controller operating from Belgium. Regardless of the targeted country being misspelled, a controller from the EU is responsible for whatever it does with personal data wherever, under the GDPR.

14. An organization is selling candy from within Europe by mail order. Does the GDPR apply?
A. Yes, because the candy is shipped within the European Union
B. Yes, it handles customers, which most likely results in the processing of personal data (correct)
C. No, because candy is not personal data
D. No, because a privacy notice is provided
Explanation: B is correct. Option A is also correct, but the explanation is wrong. C and D are just wrong.

15. To which extent is the GDPR applicable to Canadian direct marketing companies targeting EU citizens?
A. The e-Privacy directive does not apply outside of the European Union, hence there is no regulation of direct marketing
B. Only appropriate data security safeguards are required, no administrative safeguards
C. Canadian marketing requires approval of the Canadian privacy ombudsman
D. The GDPR applies to the activities targeting EU citizens (correct)
Explanation: regardless of it being a Canadian company, option D is correct.

16. Which of the following is an example of the application of the storage limitation principle?
A. Denying data subjects access after the data are no longer needed
B. Making sure the data are accurate before destroying the data
C. Not storing personal data longer than necessary for the purposes for which the data were collected (correct)
D. Performing regular audits to verify not more data than needed have been collected
Explanation: C is obvious. The others are not relevant to storage limitation.

17. Which of the following is an example of the purpose limitation principle?
A. Vetting contractors before allowing them access to the data
B. Using the personal data only for the purpose for which the data were collected (correct)
C. Using encryption methods suitable for the processing purpose
D. Denying the Corporate Information Security Officer access to the processing description
Explanation: only option B restricts the use to its purpose. The others do not necessarily result in limiting the use to only for the collection purpose.

18. Which of the following is an example of the application of confidentiality?
A. Information is only shared with the persons that need to have access to the required information for use in line with the purpose for which it was collected (correct)
B. Only publicly available personal data being used
C. Not storing any names in the collection process
D. Providing a privacy notice before collecting the data
Explanation: only option A describes something that keeps the data confidential. The other options are all nice, but do not necessarily result in confidentiality.

19. Which of the following is an example of the application of the concept accuracy?
A. Allowing data subjects to correct their data when there is a change (correct)
B. Making sure the data stay the way they were collected, regardless of data subject signals
C. Preventing data breaches that allow outsiders to access the data
D. Requiring consent for the processing of the data
Explanation: option B is the opposite. Options C and D may add to the accuracy, but option A is specifically for making data more accurate, and therefore the correct answer.

20. When is consent most likely not required?
A. When it concerns digital marketing surveys for children, with a reward at the end
B. When it concerns public sensitive data (correct)
C. When it concerns processing where no other lawful processing criterion applies
D. When it concerns data that are nice to have, but not essential for the purpose, and it differs per person whether the interests of the controller outweigh the interests of the data subject
Explanation: under option B it is not specified that it concerns personal data, only sensitive data. Even if it were sensitive personal data, when the data are public the data have likely been made public by the data subject, which causes consent not to be the only option anymore.

21. When is article 6b of the GDPR, processing for a contract of which the data subject is a part, applicable?
A. When installing CCTV in order to keep customers safe
B. When processing a CV and other required applicant details in the recruitment process (correct)
C. When processing your employees' data in the process of organizing the annual corporate family event
D. When posting the photograph of individuals that have stolen from your shop
Explanation: anything before a labor contract can be seen as a pre-contractual phase. Perhaps this is not the case in every EU country, but option B is still the best option amongst the options. Option C may seem fine, but it is highly unlikely that a family event is necessary (unless it, for example, is part of a collective labor agreement, which it likely is not).

22. When is article 6c of the GDPR, compliance with a legal obligation the controller is subject to, applicable?
A. When a school stores its potential student's addresses after sending a leaflet with information because it is legally required to provide information on the educational options it provides
B. When posting CCTV images of individuals that have stolen from your shop
C. When a school records the national personal identification number, as required by law (correct)
D. When asking a patient for consent to send him/her information regarding the medication he/she is taking
Explanation: legal obligations like C that require the processing of personal data can be performed with the lawful processing criterion 6c (legal obligation).

23. Which lawful processing criterion would you most likely use if you are asked access to provide the medical file of one of your employees by an ambulance that needs the information to treat the employee (who fell unconscious)?
A. Vital interest (correct)
B. Performance of a contract
C. Task carried out in the public interest
D. Consent (sensitive personal data)
Explanation: when protecting someone's vital interests, that is also the lawful processing criterion that can be used.

24. Which of the following is the best example of the application of the transparency principle?
A. Asking for specific consent after collecting personal data
B. Requiring consent as a condition for using a website
C. Informing data subjects of their rights of erasure
D. Providing a privacy notice explaining what is done with the collected data, by who and why (correct)
Explanation: option D is the only option that gives data subjects insight into what is done with their personal data (thus providing transparency).

Use this scenario for the following four questions:

A supermarket has a discount card which is provided free to its customers. In order to receive a discount for specific products, customers hand over the discount cart at the cash register, after which it is scanned and the discount is applied.

Besides the card being used to provide a discount, it also registers all items purchased by the user of the discount card. Through a website, users can register the card and link it to themselves in order to receive personalized discount offers, based on their shopping preferences.

The supermarket's new data protection officer has just started to familiarize himself with the discount card and the processes behind it. During his efforts to fully explore the process, he finds out no privacy notice is provided to the customers before linking their name and e-mail address to the discount card. Somewhat alarmed by this discovery, he plans a meeting with the manager in charge of the discount card rollout.

25. When should the privacy notice be provided to the customers using the discount card?
A. Before storing the name and e-mail address
B. Before asking the customer for his/her name and e-mail address (correct)
C. Before issuing the discount card
D. Before sending any personalized discounts to the customer, since this is considered marketing
Explanation: answer B is before any personal data are processed, yet close enough to when the data are going to be collected (so that the notice is relevant). For the issuing of the card, no processing of personal data is needed, so no notice is required. For options A and D, processing of personal data has already taken place.

26. What is required to be part of the privacy notice for the discount card?
A. The names and addresses of the processors used
B. The lawful processing criteria (correct)
C. The names and addresses of the sub-processors used
D. The population size of the data subjects
Explanation: lawful processing criteria are required to be part of the notice to the data subject. A and C are allowed, but only the categories of third parties are required. D is nonsense.

27. Which of the following is an example of a layered privacy notice?
A. A privacy notice on each sub-section of a website, so that the notice is always visible
B. A notice with reference to another privacy policy so that not all information is contained in just one notice
C. A notice with the contact details of the general council as well as the privacy council so that more specific communication can take place
D. A notice in which a section can be unfolded for every area of interest, such as for marketing (correct)
Explanation: only D describes layered notices. The point is that not all information is presented at once, but selectable somewhere if desired. B may seem correct, but it is just costing extra effort and perhaps makes the actual notice not comprehensive enough.

28. Which of the following elements is not required in the discount card privacy notice?
A. Contact details of the Data Protection Officer
B. A mention of who the controller is
C. A description of third parties involved
D. The contact person at the Data Protection Agency (correct)
Explanation: Although there needs to be mention of the Data Protection Authority, listing the contact person is not required. Also, it is AUTHORITY, not AGENCY. Option D provides the only option not required.

29. Which of the following is not true regarding fair processing notices?
A. Fair processing notices are held to more elaborate requirements since the GDPR
B. It is mandatory, where possible, to provide a fair processing notice before collecting personal data
C. The Data Protection Directive already specified methods for controllers to provide fair processing notices (correct)
D. The identification of the controller needs to be included in a fair processing notice
Explanation: the Data Protection Directive was not specific regarding the methods. The GDPR is more specific. Although the answer may be debatable to some extent, C is the least wrong. Questions this tricky are on the actual exam, so when you encounter them pick the least wrong answer.

30. What is true for third parties collecting personal data on behalf of a controller?
A. Neither the identity nor the contact details are required to be disclosed to the data subjects
B. The controller is exempt from the requirement to identify itself because a processor is in charge of determining the means and purpose of the collection
C. On request, the data processing agreement needs to be made available to the data subjects
D. Third parties are required to identify the controller for which the personal data are collected (correct)
Explanation: D is part of the notice requirement, which also applies when third parties collect the data on behalf of someone else.

31. Which of the following is most appropriate when it concerns technologies that provide fair processing notice challenges, such as CCTV?

A. When it is difficult to provide a fair processing notice due to the type of technology used, the most appropriate way of delivering the information in the context of the technology has to be sought (correct)

B. Difficult technologies are exempt from the requirement to provide a fair processing notice, due to the expense of the organization outweighing the data subject's right to privacy

C. CCTV is only allowed to be used with consent, meaning the fair processing notice can be provided at the same moment consent is provided

D. Difficulties need to be reported to the European Data Protection Board for approval

Explanation: difficulty does not mean the notice does not have to be provided before collecting the data. For CCTV it is difficult, but not impossible or unreasonable. C is only true sometimes, for example when the goal can also be met with less invasive means. D is nonsense.

32. How long does an organization initially have to respond to a data subject's access request?

A. One month (correct)
B. 20 days
C. 35 days
D. 10 days

Explanation: as mentioned in the GDPR, there is one month to respond to a data subject's request. Under certain circumstances, this can be extended, but initially, it is one month.

33. When can an organization refuse to comply with a request from a data subject to delete his/her personal data?
A. When the organization has not yet appointed a Data Protection Officer
B. During a busy period, an organization can refuse the request and tell the data subject he/she has to file the request again in three months
C. When there is a legal obligation to keep the data (correct)
D. When no objection has taken place at the moment of collection
Explanation: If there is a legal obligation, this is the legal processing criterion that can likely not be overridden by a data subject's objection.

34. When a data subject wishes to make use of his/her right to data portability, which of the following applies?
A. The controller has the right to prevent a data subject from providing the personal data to another controller
B. The personal data have to be provided in machine-readable format (correct)
C. The right to data portability includes non-personal data
D. A data subject wishing to make use of his/her right to data portability is obliged to provide a safe means of transferring the data, e.g. an encrypted USB drive
Explanation: B is correct, A and C are nonsense. D could be correct in certain situations, but is conditional (e.g. if the data subject has no access to the means of transfer suggested by the controller) which B is not, so on the exam B would be the correct answer.

Use this scenario for the following three questions:

A high school has received a request from Eric, who claims to be a recent graduate. Eric has started preparing his application for a scientific grant for an undergraduate research project he wants to start. In order to complete the application, he needs a transcript of his high school grades. The school still has the transcript, which it is required by law to keep for seven years.

35. What should the school do with the request?
A. Tell Eric that he was under 16 years of age at the time he attended the school, hence only his parents can be granted access
B. Ask Eric to provide identification, to make sure he is who he says he is (correct)
C. Grant the request, since the GDPR allows exceptions for scientific research
D. Refuse the request, since access requests can only be made in person
Explanation: A controller has the duty to verify the identity of the data subject before granting access to the personal data.

36. If Eric, upon realizing how poor his grades were, requests erasure of the transcript (since it concerns his personal data), what should the school do?
A. Refuse the erasure of the transcript (correct)
B. Require Eric to sign a deletion request statement, as a place holder for any legal requirement
C. Grant the request, since the GDPR gives data subjects the right to be forgotten
D. Inform Eric that only his parents are able to authorize the school to delete the transcript
Explanation: Answer A is correct because the school is legally required to keep the transcript for a period of seven years, which has not passed yet. This legal obligation is their legal processing criterion.

37. If, after refusal of access, Eric hacks the school's IT system and gains access to his transcript, which of the following is most likely the case?
A. It is fine, as Eric is merely executing his rights
B. The data have to be deleted, as required by law
C. It constitutes a data breach (correct)
D. Eric has forfeited his rights to erasure
Explanation: breaking into the IT system is a breach of security with the exposure of personal data, hence a data breach. A, B and D are nonsense.

38. What is the best example of appropriate technical and organizational measures?
A. The highest standards of IT security, with automatic updates enabled
B. Security measures appropriate for the level of risk that the processing poses, periodically re-evaluated (correct)
C. What the salesperson recommends, if you do not trust the Chief Information Security Officer's demands
D. Procedures and equipment that ensure full encryption and access to data through a single person only
Explanation: B is correct, as it suggests taking into account the level of risk. A is overkill, hence not appropriate. C is nonsense. D is about encryption, and appropriate measures are about more than encryption (in most situations).

39. What is required when contracting an external company to perform payroll operations?
A. A Data Processing Agreement (correct)
E. Binding Corporate Rules
C. Approval from the Data Protection Authority
D. If the services were provided before 2016, no additional actions are required
Explanation: An external payroll company processes personal data (information about employees' salary), hence is a processor and requires a Data Processing Agreement is required.

40. What is likely the most appropriate first step after discovering a potential data breach?
A. Starting an investigation into what exactly has been breached (correct)
B. Filing a claim against any processor at fault
C. Calling the Data Protection Authority to request help with the investigation
D. Informing all data subjects that your organization holds data on
Explanation: First things first, so it is important to determine what has been breached so any issues that require immediate action are found as soon as possible. There is a deadline for reporting to the DPA, which is option C, but minimizing the breach has the priority.

41. If a processor that you have contracted reports a data breach to you (the controller), what actions are required of you?
A. Record the breach, and potentially report it to the Data Protection Authority (correct)
B. The processor is responsible, and therefore the only one to take action
C. No action is required of the controller, as there are Binding Corporate Rules in place
D. No action is required of the controller, as there is a Data Processing Agreement in place
Explanation: As a controller, you are responsible as well, and breaches have to be recorded (at the very least). Depending on the magnitude and significance of the breach, more action can be required, such as reporting the breach to the DPA or informing the data subjects.

42. How fast is a controller required to report a severe breach to the Data Protection Authority?
A. 24 hours after finishing the investigation
B. 72 hours after having become aware of the breach (correct)
C. 24 hours after informing the involved data subjects
D. 48 hours
Explanation: answer B is the text as it appears in the GDPR.

43. If you are a processor, do you need a Data Processing Agreement for any sub-processors that you use?
A. No, any sub-processor you hire is automatically liable for complying with the Data Processing Agreements you are part of
B. Sub-processors never require a Data Processing Agreement
C. A processor is not allowed to use sub-processors, as these are required to be contracted directly through the controller
D. Yes, the Data Processing Agreement does not automatically apply to sub-processors (correct)
Explanation: D is the most likely answer. Logically you should be able to prove that a sub-processor agreed to the terms you as a processor are held to.

44. Which of the following would most likely require a Data Processing Agreement?
A. A flower service, delivering flowers to your personal address
B. A catering service, asked to provide three gluten-free meals for a company event
C. The company leasing you IT hardware for your organization
D. A cloud provider where the minutes of meeting of all meetings of your organization are stored (correct)
Explanation: minutes of meeting generally contain the names of the persons present and excerpts from their input. Hence, they contain personal data and the cloud provider is a third-party which is storing (processing) the personal data, which requires a Data Processing Agreement.

45. Within what time does a processor have to inform a controller after becoming aware of a Data Breach?
A. Within 72 hours after having become aware of it
B. 48 hours
C. 24 hours
D. Without undue delay after becoming aware of a personal data breach (correct)
Explanation: for controllers the answer would be A, but for processors the answer is D.

46. What is the most likely situation in which communication to the data subjects needs to take place?
A. An e-mail has been wrongfully addressed and contains someone's refugee status (correct)
B. Thousands of IP addresses, of persons who responded to a digital marketing survey, have been published
C. An encrypted laptop with a kill switch has been lost, leaving the backup as the only copy
D. A drawer containing a variety of documents, including business cards containing personal data randomly, spread out through the drawer, has been accessed by the after-hours cleaner
Explanation: A and D are the only options where personal data have clearly been exposed. However, D is not processing by automated means and is not contained in a filing system, hence out of the GDPR's scope.

47. Which of the following is most accurate regarding security?
A. A controller is responsible for the security of its processing, but can shift this responsibility by outsourcing it to a processor
B. A data processor is held to different security standards than a controller
C. Processor and controller both need to be able to prove they are processing with an appropriate level of security (correct)
D. No duty to inspect red flags lies with the contractor, as long as a data processing agreement has been signed
Explanation: A, B, and D are just false. Everyone is responsible.

48. Which of the following does not constitute a data breach?
A. A wrongfully addressed e-mail containing personal data
B. The accidental destruction of a securely encrypted hard drive containing personal data, which has not been backed up
C. A fully encrypted laptop containing personal data being stolen
D. Processing personal data without the required data processing agreement (correct)
Explanation: option D might be illegal processing, but it is no breach of a security measure and hence no data breach in the context of the GDPR. A wrongfully addressed e-mail may sound weird but is considered a breach.

49. What is not a good example of *privacy by design*?
A. Having the option to select "Do not Track" in a browser (correct)
B. Making sure as little information as needed is collected within a website
C. Automatically disabling analytical and tracking cookies
D. Making sure no connection with the internet is made if it is not needed
Explanation: For true privacy by design, the "Do not track" option should be functional by default. Now, it is disabled until it is selected, meaning no privacy by design.

50. When is a Data Protection Impact Assessment most likely required?
A. When re-performing a high-risk process, with different data subjects
B. When installing additional CCTV cameras
C. When developing an application for minors with a terminal illness, which they can use on their smartphone to assist in their therapy (correct)
D. When working with anonymized ultra-sensitive data
Explanation: answer C displays the most risk factors (vulnerable subjects, sensitive data, and a large group of data subjects). B could also be correct but does not mention anything about CCTV and data subjects (the CCTV could be installed to keep an eye on the organization's pets). A is not necessary, since you do not have to re-perform DPIAs for similar processing. And D is anonymous, hence the GDPR does not apply.

51. What is the best description of a Data Protection Impact Assessment?
A. A risk assessment used to come to an estimate on the needed financial resources
B. An assessment of the impact of the processing operations on the protection of personal data (correct)
C. A mandatory document for all types of processing
D. A mandatory document for high-risk data, regardless of whether the high-risk data are personal data
Explanation: A is wrong because it does not mention personal data. C's & D's scope is bigger than personal data. B is the only correct answer.

52. In which of the following cases is a Data Protection Officer not mandatory?
A. Courts acting in their judicial capacity (correct)
B. Public authorities
C. When a company engages in regular and systematic monitoring of data subjects on a large scale
D. When the core activities of the organization consist of the processing on a large scale of special categories of personal data
Explanation: see the part in the GDPR regarding the DPO. Answer A is explicitly mentioned.

53. What is not required of the Data Protection Officer?
A. Inform and advise the organization of its data protection obligations
B. Monitor compliance with the GDPR
C. Accept dismissal or penalization for the performance of his/her tasks (correct)
D. Report breaches to the Data Protection Authority
Explanation: Dismissal or penalization is forbidden for the performance of the DPO's tasks. Reporting breaches is tricky, as this is not required by the GDPR, but also not forbidden, hence organizations could require it of their DPO. There will be tricky questions like this on the exam, so try to think of the logic the creator of the exam might have used if two answers both seem correct.

54. What is the predecessor of Privacy Shield?
A. HIPAA
B. The CLOUD Act
C. Safe Harbor (correct)
D. Binding Corporate Rules
Explanation: a useless fact, but C is correct. Keep in mind that, even though it is no longer valid, you are likely still required to know about Privacy Shield and Safe Harbor.

55. What is the best description of *standard contractual clauses*?
A. A framework for transatlantic exchanges of personal data for commercial purposes between the European Union and Canada
B. Model clauses for personal data exchanges with countries outside the European Union (correct)
C. A framework for transatlantic exchanges of personal data for commercial purposes between the European Union and the rest of the world
D. It is an inter-company agreement, with at least one of the affiliates based in the United States, with approval of the designated Data Protection Authority
Explanation: B is correct, it describes standard contractual clauses (also referred to as *model clauses*).

56. What is the best description of Binding Corporate Rules?
A. A document describing the internal reprimanding of employees involved in data breaches
B. Any international document for which the Data Protection Officer has given his/her approval
C. A slimmed-down version of the standard contractual clauses
D. A legally binding document applicable to every member of a group's undertaking (correct)
Explanation: A, B & C are nonsense. BCR are a set of rules between a group's members that describe their data protection policies in a way that indicates full compliance with the GDPR.

57. Which of the following countries is not considered adequate (moment of writing, August 2020)?
A. New Zealand
B. Jersey
C. Guernsey
D. Australia (correct)
Explanation: Australia is not on the list at the moment.

58. When would standard contractual clauses for international data transfer be used (moment of writing, August 2020)?
A. When transferring data to a government agency in Canada (correct)
B. When using the service of a processor in Israel
C. When transferring to another affiliate of the same organization in a country that has not been found adequate, with Binding Corporate Rules in place
D. When transferring substantial anonymized data to a country with a recent high-profile data breach
Explanation: Canada is only deemed adequate for commercial organizations, not its government. Hence, the government is the inadequate part of Canada.

59. What is not true about standard contractual clauses?
A. When used instead of Binding Corporate Rules, each legal entity of a group has to sign the standard contractual clauses
B. Clauses can be freely adjusted to fit the specifics of the exchange (correct)
C. The clauses cannot be altered freely
D. The Data Protection Authority does not need to authorize the use of unaltered standard contractual clauses
Explanation: You cannot just change some clauses and sell them as something allowed by the European Commission for international data exchange. There has to be assurance they are appropriate, which is why additional review by the Data Protection Authority is required.

60. Which of the following is still necessary for the transfer of personal data to a country with an adequacy decision?
A. Binding Corporate Rules
B. Model clauses
C. Alternative Transfer mechanisms
D. A Data Processing Agreement, in case of processors and sub-processors (correct)
Explanation: sub-processors need to sign something to be bound by it. The GDPR might apply to them automatically, but the data processing agreement does not automatically apply (how can you prove they are aware of the content if they have not signed it?).

61. Which of the following is true for Binding Corporate Rules?
A. They have to be approved by the Data Protection Officer
B. They have to be part of a Data Processing Agreement
C. They have to be approved by the Data Protection Authority (correct)
D. They replace the need for a Data Processing Agreement
Explanation: you cannot have a set of Binding Corporate Rules that is not approved. A & B are not required by the GDPR. D is false.

62. Who determines whether a country has an adequate level of protection?
A. The European Data Protection Supervisor
B. The Data Protection Authority
C. The European Commission (correct)
D. The country's privacy ombudsperson or commissioner
Explanation: A & B have different roles. D is made up. C is the correct answer.

63. At the moment of the drafting of the GDPR, which of the possibilities it provides was new?
A. Standard contractual clauses for international data transfer
B. Sub-processor contract requirements
C. Codes of conduct for international data transfer (correct)
D. Controller to controller standard contractual clauses
Explanation: C is correct, the other options were already available prior to the GDPR.

64. For multinational organizations, what is true regarding where their Data Protection Authority is located?
A. Multinational organizations only answer to the European Data Protection Supervisor
B. Multinational organizations only answer to the European Data Protection Board
C. Multinational organizations fall outside of the scope of the GDPR, provided that their head office is in a country that has been deemed adequate
D. The supervisory authority of the main/single establishment of the controller/processor shall be competent to act as the lead supervisory authority (correct)
Explanation: D is correct, the rest is nonsense.

65. What is not a role of the Data Protection Authority?
A. Promote awareness and understanding of data protection
B. Handle complaints and carry out investigations
C. Provide tools and templates for GDPR implementation (correct)
D. Monitor development of ICT and commercial practices
Explanation: it is not obliged to provide any tools and templates. It might be, but this is not mentioned in the GDPR.

66. What is the name of the predecessor of the European Data Protection Board?
A. European Data Protection Supervisor
B. Safe Harbor Council
C. Article 29 Working Party (correct)
D. Privacy Shield Council
Explanation: a useless fact, but the correct answer. Expect a few questions regarding useless facts on the actual exam.

67. What is true regarding the European Data Protection Board?
A. It is, among others, composed of the head of one supervisory authority of each member state (correct)
B. The opinions issued by the European Data Protection Board are fully enforceable as law
C. The European Data Protection Board issues revisions of the GDPR, as needed
D. The European Data Protection Board, due to its authority and expertise, has the power to overturn any judge-made decision
Explanation: B, C, and D are nonsense.

68. What is true about the possible fines under the GDPR?
A. The maximum fine is 2% of the total worldwide annual turnover of the previous year, or 10 Million Euros
B. The maximum fine is 10 Million Euros for companies operating on a national level, and 20 Million Euros for a company operating on a global level
C. There is no maximum fine
D. The maximum fine is 4% of the total worldwide annual turnover of the previous year, or 20 Million Euros (correct)
Explanation: D is the much-talked-about correct answer.

69. Which of the following is not one of the supervisory authority's investigative powers?
A. To carry out investigations in the form of data protection audits
B. To carry out a review on certifications that demonstrate compliance
C. To fine individuals for not cooperating with an investigation (correct)
D. To obtain access to any premises of the controller and the processor
Explanation: fines cannot be issued to individuals. At least, not based on the GDPR, which is the law you are supposed to assume this question pertains to.

70. What is true regarding the compensation mentioned in article 82 of the GDPR?
A. Limited to a maximum of 4% of the global annual turnover or 20 Million Euros
B. The damage can be material or non-material (correct)
C. Limited to a maximum of 2% of the global annual turnover
D. Limited to 10 Million euros
Explanation: A, C, and D are not applicable to article 82.

71. What is the most likely legal basis for processing employee data?
A. The data subject has given consent
B. The data subject has implied consent
C. Necessary in order to protect the vital interests of the data subject
D. Necessary for the performance of a contract (correct)
Explanation: with employees, the most likely two legal processing criteria are contract, Article 6(1)(b), and legal obligation, Article 6(1)(c). C is possible, but not common. B is nonsense and A should be avoided.

72. What is true about workplace monitoring?
A. In order not to upset the employees, the cameras should be hidden
B. Approval from the Data Protection Authority is required
C. A privacy notice is required (correct)
D. Explicit consent is always required
Explanation: a privacy notice is required for any processing, where it is practically possible. D may seem correct, but is not necessarily always the case, which is why C is the correct answer. A is nonsense and B is not required.

73. Which of the following is most likely a safeguard in place when an organization allows employees to use personal devices for work?
A. Provide budget for procuring devices
B. Mandatory cloud backups of the entire device's content
C. Establish a Bring Your Own Device policy (correct)
D. Exclusion of employee devices from the data inventory
Explanation: The only solution that could provide some sort of safeguard is option C. Option A does nothing, and options B and D cause extra risks.

Use this scenario for the following three questions:

Company X is the market leader in the production of diet pills. It has a facility in Sweden, which employs 1200 people full time. Recently, t invented a drug that speeds up metabolism. This drug's formula is something company X wants to keep a secret for as long as possible.

In the coming months company X plans on expanding its manufacturing facility to create space for the production of its newest diet pill. Heavy use will be made of CCTV, especially in the critical production areas where the ingredients are mixed.

Before being allowed to work for company X, employees are informed of the use of CCTV. However, the new manufacturing area raises concerns. The works council requested an urgent meeting with the board of directors and the Data Protection Officer.

74. What is the role of an organization's works council with regards to privacy in the case of company X?
A. Works councils are mostly active in the UK, and company X is based in Sweden, hence the works council is likely going to have little power
B. Works councils are always required to be asked for approval for any privacy-related issues, so also in this case
C. The works council could be involved if privacy issues are the result of changes in the work environment (correct)
D. Works councils are responsible for the development of a whistle-blowing scheme, which makes CCTV redundant and disproportionate
Explanation: C is correct. Works councils generally have some say in these kinds of matters. A is just false, B is false and D could be the case but does not quite answer the question.

75. Company X is not asking its employees for consent for the use of CCTV. What is most likely the reason not to ask its employees for consent?
A. Because it would be difficult to be truly freely given (correct)
B. Because of the large number of consent forms
C. Because employers only process employee data based on legitimate interest
D. Because employers only process employee data for the vital interest of employees
Explanation: A is correct because employees might feel there could be consequences to not providing consent.

76. Besides the use of CCTV, there are other personal data that company X processes of its employees, potentially of a sensitive nature. When are sensitive personal data about employees allowed to be processed without consent?
A. When compensation is provided for the use of the personal data
B. When the name of the employee is replaced with a code, and the list with names belonging to the codes is kept separately
C. When the processing is carried out in the legitimate interest of the organization
D. When it is necessary for carrying out obligations in the field of employment law (correct)
Explanation: Only D is correct. B may seem somewhat correct, but replacing names with codes is only a safeguard and not something that lifts the ban on using sensitive personal data.

77. Which of the following is most likely true for an employer installing CCTV throughout the organization's premises?
A. The legitimate interest criterion is used and privacy notices are visible before entering the premises (correct)
B. The works councils have no right to provide input regarding the decision to place CCTV
C. Employers are allowed to do as they please, since coming to work is voluntary
D. Employees can request to see the recordings of all their colleagues based on their right to access
Explanation: A is the most likely. B is not likely as works councils (if they are present) have a say in these kinds of matters to some extent. C is nonsense (in Europe at least). D could be true if the requesting person is in every image and the privacy of the other employees is not disproportionately violated, which is an unlikely scenario.

78. What is necessary for the use of geolocation tracking of employees?
A. It needs to be proportional and necessary (correct)
B. The geolocation of employees does not fall under the category personal data
C. Geolocation tracking is only allowed if vehicles are tracked, and not employees
D. Within Europe, geolocation tracking is allowed without any restrictions
Explanation: A is the only correct answer. C would also be correct, if the vehicles were not also automatically revealing something about their owner/driver (expect reasoning like this on the exam).

79. What is required when sending digital direct marketing?
A. A prior customer relationship and the opportunity to opt-out (correct)
B. A data broker's list of contacts
C. Social media profile information
D. Any list provided by a third party from outside of the European Economic Area
Explanation: see the e-Privacy directive (or regulation). Only answer A makes sense. Unless the data broker has obtained all contacts legally and has obtained all the required approvals, which generally is not how data brokers operate.

80. What is required when sending direct marketing via old-fashioned snail mail?
A. Works council approval
B. A legitimate interest and a prior customer relationship (correct)
C. A follow up e-mail with the request for a confirmation of receipt
D. Approval from the Data Protection Authority
Explanation: only answer B is correct. The others are just false.

81. Which of the following is not true regarding web beacons?
A. Web beacons can be third-party trackers
B. Opt-out is sufficient, which can be provided through changing the browser settings (correct)
C. More than just the IP address can be collected when using a web beacon
D. The use of a third-party web beacon for profiling most likely requires consent
Explanation: web beacons generally collect personal data, which at the very least requires a privacy notice. Of course, there is a lack of clarity regarding what constitutes personal data in the context of a web beacon, but assuming the widespread simultaneous collection of data (e.g. linking to a social media profile), it is quite likely a web beacon can expose a lot. The opportunity to opt-out does not replace a privacy notice, or consent (if required).

82. When targeting children under 13 for an online survey, which of the following is most likely required?
A. The option to opt-out
B. The option to omit the child's address
C. Parental consent (correct)
D. A contract with the child
Explanation: many things online are likely to require parental consent. The other answers do not make sense in this context. Of course, there are situations imaginable where an online survey does not require parental consent, but the exam will have tricky questions like this, so beware of the assumptions the examiner may want you to make.

83. Which of the following is true regarding the use of photos of members of your organization for marketing purposes?
A. Using your employees' photographs is considered necessary for the performance of their employment contract
B. If your organization's members are recognizable, you will most likely require consent for the use of the photograph for marketing purposes (correct)
C. Works council approval is required
D. Only photographs that are also posted on social media are allowed to be used for marketing purposes
Explanation: using photos for marketing likely requires publishing of some sort, which is an extra step in privacy invasion and consent is most likely the only possible lawful processing criterion. Of course, the assumption here is that the persons are still alive, which is the kind of assumption you are required to make throughout the entire exam.

84. Which of the following is true regarding the use of publicly available data for marketing purposes?
A. Publicly available information falls outside of the scope of the GDPR
B. For any processing of publicly available information, one of the lawful processing criteria will have to be met (correct)
C. When first processing the publicly available information outside of Europe, it will fall outside of the scope of the GDPR
D. Only information publicly available in Europe falls under the scope of the GDPR
Explanation: A, C, and D are nonsense. B is correct.

85. What is the best description of cloud computing?
A. The hosting of intranet pages that are not accessible to outsiders
B. The use of dynamic IP addresses
C. Any storage of data on an externally hosted server (correct)
D. Phone towers connecting individual devices
Explanation: the answers are posed somewhat misleadingly, as will be the case on the actual exam. Only answer C depicts something stored on the internet (which is a very simplified definition).

86. Which of the following types of cookies least likely requires consent?
A. Tracking cookies
B. Web beacons
C. Functional Cookies (correct)
D. Analytical cookies
Explanation: tracking technologies and web beacons generally collect personal data. Analytical cookies could collect personal data. Functional cookies are allowed.

87. Regarding social networks, which of the following is most likely true?
A. Any processing a social media site does falls under personal use
B. Only the processing of photos depicting race or physical impairment requires consent
C. An individual is always regarded to have provided valid implicit consent
D. Consent is required for organizations to transfer personal data to social networks for marketing purposes (correct)
Explanation: D is correct, consent is likely the only lawful processing criterion for this. A case for legitimate interest could be made, but not a very strong one, especially given the lack of control/clarity and weak arguments for necessity.

88. Which of the following is true regarding search engine operators?
A. Data retention periods must be proportional (correct)
B. Search engine operators require consent before processing search commands
C. Search engines are always considered to be processors
D. Search engines fall outside the scope of the GDPR
Explanation: A is correct, B is likely not the case and the other two options are false.

89. Which of the following is most likely true regarding a well-known social media site's practice of labeling its members' sexual preferences based on their online behavior?
A. Any online behavior is manifestly made public, so any conclusions regarding sexual preference attached to it do not require consent
B. The website needs to obtain consent to record a prediction/inference of someone's sexual preference (correct)
C. Inference is fine, as it is not 100% certain to be accurate
D. Unless the data subject objects, the accuracy principle is not enforceable since the data are not presented as accurate
Explanation: recording personal data, whether it is accurate or not, is subject to the requirements of the GDPR. In other words, made-up data about actual persons is also to be considered personal data. Also, public personal data are still in the scope of the GDPR.

90. Which of the following is not true regarding privacy notices and social media?
A. The privacy notice needs to be concise and in an easily accessible form
B. Transparency is a requirement of the privacy notice
C. The privacy notice always needs to be intelligible
D. The consequences of actions on social media are commonly known, and for that reason do not require a privacy notice (correct)
Explanation: despite consequences being commonly known, they still have to be communicated.

Made in the USA
Columbia, SC
14 February 2022